KU-371-352

Truly Foul & Cheesy™

Kings and Queens Facts

& Jokes

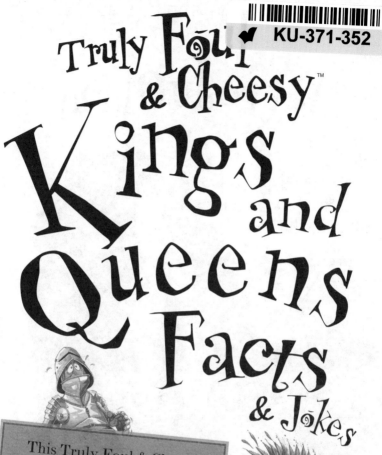

This Truly Foul & Cheesy
book belongs to:

....

Written by

John Townsend

Illustrated by

David Antram

BOOK HOUSE
a SALARIYA imprint

Introduction

My king-size curls show I'm the hair to the throne.

4

Disclaimer: The author really hasn't made anything up in this book (apart from some daft limericks and jokes).

He checked out the foul facts as best he could and even double-checked the fouler bits to make sure – so please don't get too upset if you find out something different from a passing princess, a royal historian professor or a court jester joKING expert.

Warning – reading this book might not make you LOL (laugh out loud) but it could make you GOL (groan out loud), feel sick out loud or SEL (scream even louder). If you are reading this in a library by a SILENCE sign… get ready to be thrown out!

If I had my way, I'd RATIFY the lot!

Official

Warning

This book takes a quick peek through the castle gates and palace windows into the secret chambers of the high and mighty from the past. As a regal romp round revolting royals, it digs up the dirt left by the most powerful men and women who ever ruled in different countries. We find their dirty washing and hang it out for all to see the grubby gussets, as well as amusing, interesting and scintillating snippets. Some are particularly foul and cheesy. You have been warned...

Loopy limerick

Of the kings and the queens we have known,
How many were foul to the bone?
In charge of an army
Some monarchs went barmy
Just as soon as they sat on the throne.
(Power can corrupt, some have shown!)

I can do just what I like.

Riddles

First up – time to get some cheesy riddles out of the way...

Q: What do Richard the Lionheart, Queen of the
    Nile and Winnie the Pooh have in common?
A: The same middle name.

Q: What has six legs, four ears
    and a shining suit of armour?
A: A king on horseback.

Q: What is the first thing a king or queen
    does when they come to the throne?
A: They sit down.

Q: When is a piece of wood like an
    ancient king or queen?
A: When it's an old ruler.

Q: When does a queen get very wet?
A: When she becomes the raining monarch.

I wonder how long this reign will last.

Trickier riddles

Who am I?

Kings and queens may cling to power,
While jesters often fall
Yet, when the game of thrones turns sour,
The lowest may trump them all.
Answer: An ace (in a pack of cards)

Jester a little song for your majesty.

Who was it?

One night, a king and a queen walked into an empty castle. The next day the king, the queen and someone else walked out. What happened? Answer: One 'knight', a king and a queen walked out.

Where was it?

One knight, a king and a queen moved around a castle. The floor had to be carefully checked – why? Answer: It was a chess board.

Who are we?

A king, queen and two twins are in a large room. How are there no adults in the room? Answer: Because they're all beds.

Did you know?

A king or queen is the chief authority over a country and its people. In the past, in particular, kings and queens were rich, powerful and to be feared by all, especially commoners. Today's kings and queens tend to be national figureheads, rather than the ruthless rulers from history. There are still over 20 monarchies in the world – kings, queens, sultans, emperors and emirs who reign over various countries. In a constitutional monarchy, the monarch's power is limited by a constitution (a government's democratic rules). But in an absolute monarchy, the monarch has unlimited power. Some of that power in the past could be very scary.

HAAAAAAAA

For the record

The Japanese monarchy is the world's oldest, having ruled for over 2,600 years. Crown Prince Naruhito will become the next emperor in 2019. The British monarchy is almost half that age, but is still one of the oldest in the world. Many other monarchies came to grisly ends in revolutions which got rid of their kings and queens. It wasn't always luxury and riches being a monarch. Heads often rolled... with a sickening thud.

King of Pigs

The first kings in Britain weren't so much kings as local chiefs. We don't know much about the ancient Celtic leaders, although one seemed to be quite a character. King Bladud (apparently the father of King Lear, made famous in the play by William Shakespeare) decided he wanted to fly, sometime around 850 BC.

What can I call a play about a king? I'm completely throne.

AAAAAAAAAAAHHHHHHHH

The story goes that he strapped a hefty pair of wings to his arms and jumped. Result = SPLAT. Dead. However, before his fall from power, he and his pigs allegedly discovered the healing springs of Bath, England. The Romans later made them famous (the baths, not the pigs). Today you can visit the town of Bath, its Roman baths and glimpse a statue of King Bladud and the occasional model pig.

Queen of Celts

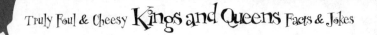

When the Romans invaded Britain in 43 AD, they didn't expect to meet a Celtic queen with attitude. In 60 AD, Queen Boudicca of the Iceni tribe raised an army to attack the Romans. Her forces went on a rampage, burning the Roman towns of Colchester and London, before heading north to St Albans.

- When the Roman army heard about this, they turned back from their campaign in Wales to face Boudicca. Even though the Romans were outnumbered by Boudicca's 200,000 warriors, they were better trained with better armour. Both sides clashed in a fierce battle. The result – Romans 1, Britons 0. Boudicca dead. She probably killed herself to avoid capture. About 70,000–80,000 people in total were killed in the battles led by Boudicca. Maybe she was just enraged that her name was given so many different spellings – from Boadicea to Boudica. No wonder she got grumpy.

Welcome to peaceful Colchester.

Fast facts

1 The Romans left Britain in 410 AD, making way for the next foreign invaders, the Saxons. They arrived in about 450 AD, and by 600 AD England was split into small Anglo-Saxon kingdoms, each ruled by a separate king. Things got extra nasty with Viking invasions around 800 AD...

Head off back home!

Well, you did tell me to 'gallop ahead'.

2 You don't want to know this

A Viking leader who ruled Scotland's Orkney Islands in the late 800s had a scary name (Sigurd Eysteinsson) and he came to a yucky end. Being a fierce fighter, he battled his way around Scotland before having a punch-up with Maelbrigt Earl of Scots. Sigurd cut off his enemy's head and kept it as a souvenir – strapped to his saddle. As he galloped from the battlefield, the severed head slammed against Sigurd's leg and a tooth dug into him. The wound quickly became infected, killing the Viking ruler. Imagine being bitten to death by a dead head. Don't you hate it when that happens?

3 Next up – enter French invaders at Hastings in 1066. Or, to put all that in a nutshell sonnet:

In England, fighting mobs rampaged,
So Saxon leaders were engaged
To wield strong force for law and order
Within each territory's border.
Brave fighting men were duly crowned
To rule each kingdom all around.
Then, after several hundred years
Of battling Viking mutineers,
The powers in English politics
Were shaken in Ten-Sixty-Six
When everything came to a head,
For Saxon Harold (king) saw red...
(literally!)
With arrow in his eye, the French
Invaded England – what a wrench!

20

OUVCCCHH!

So now, William (the conqueror from Normandy) became King William the First of England.

4 Meanwhile, in Scotland, the royals were up to all sorts of punch-ups. Spot the one queen in this list. You might know something about the foul deeds of one of the kings – from Shakespeare's 'Scottish Play'.

Killing King Duncan got me the top job.

Scotland's early monarchs

King/Queen	Length of reign	Cause of death
Malcolm II	1005–1034	Killed in battle
Duncan I	1034–1040	Killed in battle with Macbeth
Macbeth	1040–1057	Killed in battle with Malcolm III
Lulach	1057–1058	Assassinated
Malcolm III	1058–1093	Killed by steward
Duncan II	1094	Murdered
Donald III	1093–1097	Blinded/imprisoned/killed
Edgar	1097–1107	Possibly murdered
Alexander I	1107–1124	Unknown (aged 46)
David I	1124–1153	'Peacefully' (aged 69)
Malcolm IV	1153–1165	Bone disease (aged 24)
William I	1165–1214	'Old Age' (aged 71 – that was old then!)
Alexander II	1214–1249	Fever (aged 50)
Alexander III	1249–1286	Fell from a cliff
Margaret	1286–1290	Seasickness (aged 7)
John I	1292–1296	Abdicated and died in French castle
Robert I	1306–1329	Leprosy (aged 54)

Joke time

A Scottish king was much loved by his people, so they built a castle for him and his queen. Being very poor, his subjects could only afford to build it out of grass. So they worked for weeks and finally completed a lovely woven grass castle in the mountains. The king was very pleased. The English decided to present a peace offering of an ornate throne. The king accepted this gift graciously and was most pleased. The only trouble was that the throne was very uncomfortable.

So the king got himself a much more comfortable Scottish chair and kept the massive English monstrosity in the castle attic. Alas, one night the heavy throne fell through the floor and killed the king and queen. The moral of this story: PEOPLE WHO LIVE IN GRASS HOUSES SHOULDN'T STOW THRONES. Get it?

That joke has made me sick.

Has anyone got a tin-opener?

Q: Where did the kings'
knights go to eat dinner?
A: To an All-Knight Diner.

Q: Where did Scottish kings
and queens get crowned?
A: On the head.

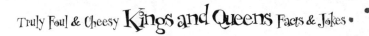

Q: Why did the Queen put a bank machine in every castle?
A: For knightly deposits.

My money worries cause sleepless knights.

Memory test

History lessons in British schools once made small children learn lists and dates of all the kings and queens. Reciting over 40 of them in the right order from memory, with a whack of the ruler for every mistake, could be very scary. So now it's time for you to suffer. You may just be able to impress your history teacher by using a rhyme to help (possibly). The verses should make sense when you see the list afterwards. Here goes...

One whack for each King Henry.

William, William, Henry, Stee,
Henry, Rich, John, Henry Three,
One-To-Three Eds, Richard Two,
Henrys Four-Five-Six... then who?

Edwards Four-Five, Rich the Baddie,
Two Henrys, Edward Six (the laddie),
Mary, Lizzie, James and then
Charlie, Charlie, James again...

Will and Mary, next Anne Gloria,
Four Georges, William, then Victoria,
Edward Seven, next-up then
George the Fifth in 1910...

Ed the Eighth soon abdicated,
So George the Sixth was coronated,
Till longest-reigning Lizzie Two
And that, for now, will have to do.

In other words:

Normans

King	Length of Reign
William I	1066–1087
William II	1087–1100
Henry I	1100–1135
Stephen	1135–1154

Plantagenets

King	Length of Reign
Henry II	1154–1189
Richard I	1189–1199
John	1199–1216
Henry III	1216–1272
Edward I	1272–1307
Edward II	1307–1327
Edward III	1327–1377
Richard II	1377–1399

I'll never remember that lot - how frustRATing!

House of Lancaster

King	Length of Reign
Henry IV	1399–1413
Henry V	1413–1422
Henry VI	1422–1461

House of York

King	Length of Reign
Edward IV	1461–1483
Edward V	1483
Richard III	1483–1485

Tudors

King	Length of Reign
Henry VII	1485–1509
Henry VIII	1509–1547
Edward VI	1553–1558
Mary I	1553–1558
Elizabeth I	1558–1603

Och, our roots are in bonnie Scotland. Guid gear comes in sma' bulk.

Stuarts

King	Length of Reign
James I	1603–1625
Charles I	1625–1649
Charles II	1660–1685
James II	1685–1688
William III	1689–1702
Mary II	1689–1694
Anne	1702–1714

Sprechen sie Deutsch?

House of Hanover

King	Length of Reign
George I	1714–1727
George II	1727–1760
George III	1760–1820
George IV	1820–1830
William IV	1830–1837
Victoria	1837–1901

Saxe-Coburg-Gotha

King	Length of Reign
Edward VII	1901–1910

One is named after a castle.

Windsor

King	Length of Reign
George V	1910–1936
Edward VIII	1936–1936
George VI	1936–1952
Elizabeth II	1952–

Quirky queens and Curious kings

The trouble with being a king or queen is that you don't need to be the best person for the job. You just have to belong to the royal family. A problem with royal families through history was that they either hated each other or tended to marry each other (or both), without much 'healthy new blood' for the baby princes and princesses. As a result, some royal babies grew up to have genetic health defects – sometimes making them act strangely. A few were called 'mad' when there was little understanding about mental health or the effects of stress. Maybe the strain of having so much power, while being at constant risk of assassination, made some monarchs act bizarrely. Try some of these...

1 King Charles VI of France

(1368–1422) was known as 'Charles the Mad'. That may be because he thought he was made of glass. No one could touch him in case he shattered! Even though he might sometimes howl like a wolf, he demanded quiet and insisted all the windows in his palace remained shut and anyone who approached him had to do so on tip-toe. Imagine thinking you're a sheet of glass – what a pane!

2 ## Queen Juana I of Castile, Spain

(1479–1555) became known as 'Joan the Mad'. At the age of 16, she married 'Philip the Handsome' of Austria, who seemed to make her act oddly (maybe his name annoyed her). When he died in his twenties, she didn't just lose the plot, she dug it up. Yes, she unearthed his coffin and took it around with her everywhere. She wouldn't let her husband's remains out of her sight. Philip the Handsome was now Philip the Corpse! When Juana refused to take a bath or sleep in a bed, her father had her taken away for treatment.

3 ## Eric XIV of Sweden

(1533–1577) was both nasty and cruel. He believed that everyone around him was plotting to kill him, so he often had innocent people executed, just for looking at him. Waving his sword, he would stalk the corridors of the castle, looking for someone to find fault with and to kill. Another of his hobbies was sending Queen Elizabeth I of England love letters which 'greatly entertained her'. Eventually, his rages and killings got too much so his half-brother had him locked-up. A delicious bowl of pea soup laced with arsenic soon put an end to the monstrous monarch Eric. Death by soup – rest in peas.

40

4 Britain's King George III

(1738–1820) had a mental illness, probably caused by a genetic disease. His behaviour became very weird and doctors didn't know how to help him. He sometimes spoke for many hours without stopping and claimed to talk to angels. Often, he'd end every sentence with the word 'peacock' or imagined he was dead. Historians don't know exactly what caused George's illness in the final half of his reign. Scientists recently tested some of George III's hair, and the results showed high levels of arsenic, which may have worsened the king's repeated bouts of 'madness'. The arsenic may have come from his powdered wigs or from the medicine his doctors gave him in the hope of making him better.

5 Christian VII of Denmark

(1749–1808) became King of Denmark and Norway at the age of 16. Within a year, he married his 15-year-old cousin, Caroline, although he said he didn't love her. Not a good start to the wedding. In fact, he said and did a lot of weird things. During dinners, he would throw food at guests. Food fights at dinner got worse when he would smack people round the face for no reason.

Once Christian threw a bowl of sugar over his grandmother's head, as well as stuck pins in the seat of her throne to make her jump and squeal. When visitors came and bowed, he'd leapfrog over their backs. Christian sometimes rampaged through the streets of Copenhagen, smashing up shops as he went. He'd often return home with black eyes, bruises and cuts. Then, to show how brave he was, he would burn his flesh and rub salt into his own wounds, then bash his head against the wall. Please don't try this at home.

Weeeeeee!

6 Catherine the Great

was Empress of Russia from 1762–1796. No Russian woman had ever reigned as long as her. Her first husband was Emperor Peter III (1728–1762), but she soon discovered he could be very childish and something of a nincompoop.

One day, after spending hours setting up all his toy soldiers in neat rows around the royal bedroom, he saw a rat pop up and chew the head off one of them. In a rage, the silly Czar grabbed the rat and held his own military court to condemn it to death. The rat was found guilty of treason and hanged on a tiny gallows he'd built especially.

Catherine described Peter as an idiot and, after being married for only six months, she had him arrested and executed (as you do). She seemed to enjoy life a little more after that, yet a rumour told of her expiring on the toilet 34 years later. Yes, she died while still on the throne.

I'm innocent – he's telling tails.

Right royal rotters

Monstrous monarchs with power to do just what they liked could be cruel and evil. These are just a few whose deeds were dastardly despicable.

King John

(1166–1216)

King John was an English king who is now seen as a wicked villain. Maybe he was more useless than evil, although he could be very cruel. His habit of having people killed forced an uprising against him, after which he was forced to sign the Magna Carta. The pope judged him too evil to remain a Roman Catholic so he had him thrown out of the church. When a bishop argued with King John, the all-powerful monarch simply had the bishop wrapped in lead and left to die. No wonder John subsequently became the main villain in traditional Robin Hood tales.

The king mis-lead me.

Do you know how archers keep fit?

Arrow-bics.

When English barons invited the French to invade and overthrow their king, John fled, and died of dysentery – apparently after gorging himself on peaches and drinking too much cider. No wonder these words were written about him a few years later: 'Foul as it is, hell itself is made fouler by the presence of King John.'

Richard III
(1452-1485)

Another baddie English king (the villain in a Shakespeare play) was Richard III. One of the reasons Richard became despised was the way he would get rid of anyone in his way to power, including his own young nephews. As he didn't want 12-year-old Edward V or his younger brother ever to become kings, Richard locked the two royal children in the dreaded Tower of London. Surprise, surprise, when Richard was crowned king in 1483, the two princes had disappeared – never to be seen again. Just two years later, he was killed in the Battle of Bosworth Field during the War of the Roses in 1485. In 2012 (527 years later), archaeologists uncovered Richard's body in a shallow grave under a Leicester car park.

OOOCH!

Ivan IV
(1533–1584)

Ivan IV ruled Russia from 1533 to 1584, from the age of three. As if that wasn't tricky enough for little Ivan, he was called Ivan the Terrible, which didn't help his self-esteem (to be fair, he earned that name after he grew up). Although Ivan made some improvements to his country during his reign, he is remembered mostly for his cruelty. Even as a boy, Ivan was said to be nasty, torturing small animals, drinking beer and throwing pets out of the Kremlin's upper windows. Still not convinced he was terrible?

You must think I'm Terrible.

He had eight wives (not all at once) and killed most of them, as well as his son by hitting him on the head with a stick. Ivan said it was an accident. Yeah – easily done. By the end of his life, Ivan was foul-tempered and was blamed for having thousands of his subjects murdered. One writer reported Ivan 'foamed at the mouth like a horse'. He died playing chess – the end of a chequered career.

Ivan idea it's all over.

51

Queen Ranavalona I
(1782–1861)

Queen Ranavalona I (1782–1861) was known as the Mad Monarch of Madagascar.

As one of the cruellest queens in history, Ranavalona ruled the African island of Madagascar with terror for 33 years. Thousands of her people died because of her brutal reign and her delight in torture and execution. She came up with scary ways to get rid of anyone who was foreign or a Christian. They were flung from cliffs, boiled in water, poisoned or beheaded. Anyone accused could be forced to drink the poisonous juice of a plant. If they survived, they were innocent. If they didn't, they were dead!

I call the Queen's poison 'royal-tea' (royalty).

It's time to head-off now, your majesty.

Other prisoners had to eat three pieces of chicken skin before swallowing a poisonous nut that caused them to vomit (if it didn't kill them). If all three pieces were not found in their vomit, the prisoner was executed. How sickening. After one battle, Ranavalona cut off her enemies' heads, stuck them on pikes and lined them up on the beach as a warning to others. It was estimated that 20,000 to 30,000 were killed each year during her gruesome reign.

Mortal monarchs

12 kings who met foul ends

1 Death by unmentionables

King Edmund II, known as Edmund Ironside, was king of England in 1016. His short rule of about 7 months could have lasted many happy years had he not needed the toilet on his travels. The story goes that Edmund had to leave a battle and use one of the latrines perched over a ditch. Little did he know that a Viking was hiding below with a long sharp spear. Just as Edmund lowered himself onto the toilet, the Viking stabbed the king twice up the bottom. King Edmund II died there and then 'on the throne'. It seems Edmund Ironside became Edmund Backside. Ouch!

DOINGG!

② Death by sitting down

King Béla I of Hungary was a warrior-king, known for being tough and strong. But how the mighty can fall. Béla's seat of power let him down – literally. In 1063, he plonked down on his wooden throne, which collapsed in bits under him. He fell so badly that his injuries got the better of him and he died of his wounds.

3 Death by saddle-sore

King William I of England was the French duke who invaded Britain in 1066 – known as William the Conqueror. After 21 years as England's king, he met a foul end. In 1087, William was doing what he loved best – leading men into battle, sitting astride a horse. When his horse bucked, William was thrown forward onto part of his saddle which 'ruptured his organs'. He died a few days later in agony. But worse was to come. As monks prepared his body for burial, they had to stuff William's over-large body into a narrow coffin. As they pushed down the corpse, William's bowels burst, filling the room with a disgusting smell. William the Pong-queror?

I'm feeling a bit eel.

4 Death by eels

King Henry I of England (the son of William the Conqueror) ruled with an iron fist but he had a weakness – eating lampreys, an eel-like blood-sucking fish. After a lamprey feast in 1135, at the age of about 66, the king looked a bit odd and promptly died. It was reported like this: 'Henry stopped at St. Denys in the wood of Lions to eat some lampreys, a fish he was very fond of, though they always disagreed with him, and the physicians had often cautioned him against eating them, but he would not listen to their advice. This food mortally chilled the old man's blood and caused a sudden and violent illness against which nature struggled and brought on an acute fever.' Moral of the story – always listen to your doctor and lay off the fish and chips in France.

5 Death by barbecue

Charles II ruled the kingdom of Navarre, Spain between 1343 and 1387. According to one account of his death, Charles was very ill, and his doctor ordered him to be completely wrapped from neck to toe in linen cloth soaked in brandy (don't ask!). One of the doctor's assistants sewed up the cloth tightly and went to cut the last piece of thread. She didn't want to use scissors in case she cut the king, so she reached for a candle to burn off the remaining thread. Oops. The linen was completely soaked in brandy, so the whole lot went up like a Christmas pudding. The mummified, flame-grilled king was burnt to a frazzle.

I'll soak you in brandy to warm you up, your highness.

6 Death by Chuckles

A king of Sicily, known as Martin of Aragon, was killed by a joke. In 1401 he'd just eaten a whole goose (something kings often did) but it gave him a bout of nasty indigestion (and probably a few goose-bumps). So, he went up to his bedroom and called for his jester to come and cheer him up with a funny joke. Apparently, the funny story was about a deer hanging by its tail from a tree after eating figs. It must have been hilarious the way the jester told it and Martin couldn't stop laughing. In fact, he laughed uncontrollably for three hours, eventually falling out of bed. When he hit the floor, he was dead. At least he died happy.

Hahahahaha!

 ## Death by sewer

James I, King of Scotland 1406–1437 was in his
royal apartment when a gang broke in to get
him. He had just enough time to hide in a smelly
sewer tunnel, but his exit was blocked and his
attackers stabbed him to death. His assassin,
Sir Robert Graham, is said to have screamed: 'I
have slain and delivered you of so cruel a tyrant,
the greatest enemy that Scotland might have.'

BANG!!

8 Death by backfire

James II, King of Scotland 1437–1460 took charge after his father (James 1) was murdered. He had a tough job trying to manage all the rival Scottish clans. They were violent times. In 1460, James wanted to celebrate a successful siege at Roxburgh Castle in the Scottish Borders. What better way than to fire a salute with giant cannons? The king stood proudly behind a cannon as the fuse was lit but after a fizz and crackle… the whole lot backfired and killed him in a jet of smoke. If only they'd done a health and safety risk assessment.

9 Death by tennis

Charles VIII of France was born in 1470, became king at the age of 12 and died in 1498, aged 28. He is remembered for how he died in his keenness to watch a tennis match. Dashing out through the door, King Charles bashed his head on the lintel and down he went. He fell into a coma and died. Game, set and match.

Between royal court and tennis court, he was well and truly caught.

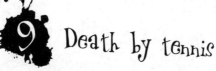

10 Death by lack of head

Charles I of England (1600–1649) has gone down in history as the king who lost his head for his beliefs. He believed strongly that God gave him absolute power to rule, however he wanted. Parliament thought otherwise, and many big quarrels developed. In 1624, the two sides went into battle and the English Civil War began. Charles I was finally defeated in 1645, imprisoned and sentenced to death for treason. His opponents were led by Oliver Cromwell, who took control of England when the monarchy was abolished. As he was led to the scaffold, King Charles wore thick underwear, so he wouldn't shiver, as he didn't want the crowd to think he was scared.

It was said that when the axe came down and sliced through his neck, a sickening groan went up through the crowd. One observer described it as 'such a groan by the thousands present, as I never heard before and I desire I may never hear again.' Spectators could go up to the scaffold and, after paying, dip handkerchiefs in his blood as it was thought the blood of a king when wiped onto a wound would cure illness.

The next day, the king's head was sewn back onto his body, which was then put in a lead coffin. Oliver Cromwell died in 1658 but three years later, his body was dug up to go on trial. Royalists found him guilty of treason and 'executed' him. Off came his dead head. Job done!

You're dead guilty.

And a smelly old rotter!

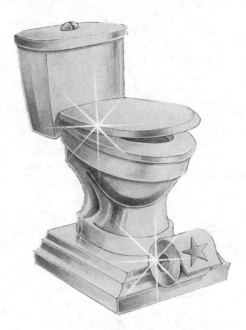

Death by lavatorial strain

King George II of Great Britain (born in Germany in 1683) died on his toilet in 1760 at the age of nearly 77 – having lived longer than any of his British predecessors. He had become rather plump, blind in one eye and hard of hearing but 'rose as usual at six and drank his chocolate' as he did every day. Then it was the usual visit to the 'royal closet' where he died mid-poo. The king was pronounced dead from 'over-exertions on the privy'. He was obviously dying to go.

12 Death by pud

A king of Sweden called Adolph Frederick (1710–1771) became known as 'the king who ate himself to death' because he ended up with massive stomach ache after eating a giant meal consisting of lobster, caviar, sauerkraut, cabbage soup, smoked herring, champagne and 14 servings of his favourite dessert: semla, a bun filled with marzipan and warm cream. Some say he got his just desserts! His insides just couldn't cope with being so stuffed, and he died of industrial-strength indigestion.

I'll finish with my favourite pud – death by chocolate.

Just for the record

In case you were wondering, the possibility of being killed was an occupational hazard for kings and queens, especially in Britain. Including the Scottish monarchy, a total of 17 monarchs in the British Isles have been murdered, assassinated or executed away from the battlefield, making it a high-risk job. Would you fancy being a monarch?

The risk assessment paperwork for being queen is frightful.

More silly riddles

Q: How do you find a princess in the forest?
A: You follow her 'foot prince'.

Q: What's it called when a King and Queen have no children?
A: A receding heir line.

Q: Why did everyone around King Arthur's table have insomnia?
A: There were lots of sleepless knights.

Terrifying Tudors

For over one hundred years, the family who ruled England were the Tudors. They were in power from 1485, when Henry Tudor was crowned King Henry VII, until the time Queen Elizabeth I died in 1603. It was a time when anyone (including several queens) could be given the chop.

Limerick

King Henry the eighth was dead scary
And so was his daughter, Queen Mary.
Whatever you did,
They'd order, 'Get rid'.
So everyone had to be wary.

King Henry VIII

King Henry VIII (born 1491, died 1547) was well known for having people close to him beheaded if they upset him. His second wife, Anne Boleyn, was only 29 when Henry decided to get rid of her. In 1536 Anne was taken to Tower Green at the Tower of London. She slowly climbed up all the steps to the scaffold to meet her executioner dressed in black. Anne spoke to the invited audience before kneeling with a blindfold. The executioner raised his sword and beheaded her with one blow. Legend has it that her lips were still moving when they lifted her head from the straw.

King Henry sneakily contrived
To six wives he'd be wedded.
One sadly died, and one survived,
Two divorced, and two beheaded.
But not in that order.

Which wife was worst
at archery? Catherine
of Arrow Gone.

The endings of the six marriages
of King Henry VIII can be
remembered by the rhyme:

'Divorced, Beheaded, Died,
Divorced, Beheaded, Survived.'

His other wife to be beheaded
was Anne Boleyn's cousin,
Katherine Howard (in 1542).

74

Catherine of Aragon
(Divorced)

Anne Boleyn
(Beheaded)

Jane Seymour
(died)

Anne of Cleves
(divorced)

Catherine Howard
(beheaded)

Catherine Parr
(survived)

75

Q: What did Anne Boleyn's mother say when her daughter said that she had fallen in love with Henry VIII?

A: Don't get too serious... that man's not worth losing your head over.

Q: Which king felt a fraction of his former self?

A: Henry 1/8th.

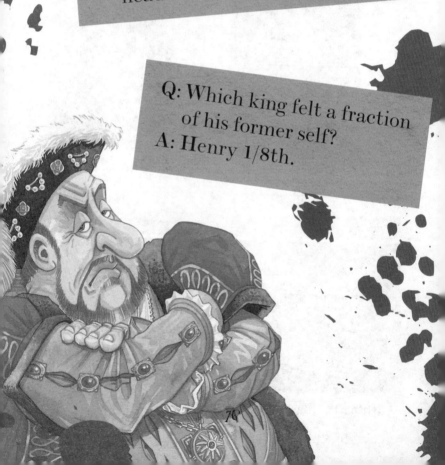

Q: Why did Henry VIII have so
many wives?
A: He liked to chop and change.

The Royal Family moved
into our neighbourhood.
They live Tudors down.

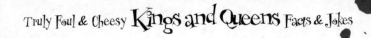

Royal rows and fearsome fights

King Henry VIII was furious that he was told what to do by the head of the Roman Catholic Church – the Pope. By making himself the head of the Church of England, Henry could then marry who he liked. Problem solved. But anyone who dared to question him would be executed for treason (which was basically for anything the king didn't like).

You'd better not be a girl.

One reason why Henry swapped his wives was because he wanted a son, rather than his two daughters (he didn't think girls would be any good to take over from him). At last baby Edward was born to wife number three (Jane Seymour), who promptly died. Never mind – heartbroken Henry simply married again.

I reckon it's time to get another wife.

Foul alert...

As King Henry VIII grew older, larger and even grumpier, all around him had to beware. He sent more men and women to their deaths than any other monarch – probably well over 50,000 people. If his foul temper wasn't bad enough, his smell was probably foul, too.

Which of my wives went crackers?

Anne of Cheese.

Henry's hygiene

– a quick peep into the king's bathroom

Henry VIII bathed at Hampton Court (one of his palaces in England) with heated water pumped in from a stove in the next room. As he grew fatter with old age, his legs gave way and he had to be carried to his bath. To ease the pain in his sore legs, his bathwater had a mixture of herbs, musk and civet added. Civet is a small cat that is supposed to give a pongy oil. Then he went to bed with a piece of fur so that fleas and lice would jump on it and not on his royal skin. But if he smelt like a dead civet, it may not have worked!

What's bugging you?

I'm itching to go to bed.

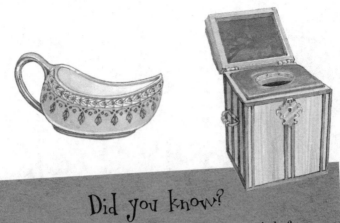

Did you know?

It was a great honour to do an intimate job for the king or queen – to look after all the royal bodily functions and washing. This revolting Tudor job was called the Groom of the King's Close Stool (or just Groom of the Stool for short), which Henry VIII created so he could be assisted with his royal bowel movements – in other words, he had his own toilet assistant. Yes, the groom of the stool was a royal bottom-wiper. Ah well, to get a good job with a monarch, you usually have to start at the bottom.

The word 'Stool' referred to a portable commode which would have been carried around at all times, along with water, towels and a wash bowl. To ensure he was carrying out his job properly, the Groom of the Stool would have to monitor the king's diet and mealtimes, then organise the day around the king's expected 'motions'.

83

1553: Edward VI died aged 15 of TB.

Tudor trials

King Henry went into decline
And died, so sickly son, aged nine
Became the King, but didn't last;
He died before six years had passed.
Half-sister Mary filled his shoes
(But only after some bad news)

1547: Henry VIII died aged 55.

84

1554: Lady Jane Grey beheaded (aged 16) with her husband, Lord Dudley (aged 18).

For their poor royal Cousin Jane,
Who'd just been crowned – a nine-day reign,
Before mean Mary sent her away
For head-chop – no more Jane Grey.
Once Bloody Mary was in charge,
She made the Roman Church enlarge.
She wanted Catholics to thrive,
Unlike when father was alive.

Queen Mary I reigned 1553-1558.

Quarrelsome Cousin queens

Having queens on the English throne was unheard of and seemed outrageous – until several queens came along at once, all related and wanting the top job. That meant only one thing – more heads would roll.

I only said I didn't like the pope.

Mary Tudor
(1516-1558)

Queen Mary I of England was the daughter of King Henry VIII and his first wife, Catherine of Aragon. Mary reigned as Queen of England for five gruesome years from 1553 until her death in 1558. Catholics and Protestants were squabbling more than ever and Mary made things even worse. She was a Catholic and put many Protestants to death, which is why she was called Bloody Mary. When she died, her half-sister, Elizabeth, became queen (a Protestant).

Upset me and you're toast!

Elizabeth I (1533–1603)

Spluttern!

Queen Elizabeth was the daughter of Anne Boleyn and Henry VIII. She was Queen of England from 1558 to 1603 and in all that time hundreds of people were executed – many of them women accused of being witches. Elizabeth was known for swearing a lot and her foul language was something she apparently inherited from her father – as well as executing people, like her own cousin from Scotland.

Mary Queen of Scots
(1542-1587)

This Mary (not to be confused with her cousin, Bloody Mary) was Queen of Scotland but she wanted to be Queen of England too, instead of cousin Elizabeth. It wasn't a good idea to be a threat to a bossy cousin. Queen Elizabeth happily signed Mary's death warrant, so in 1587 Mary Queen of Scots was led to the chopping block.

What would you like for your dinner?

Just a wee chop.

Cross alert -

Mary was blindfolded as she knelt on a velvet
cushion and rested her head on the wooden
block. The axe was raised, all gasped and…
THWACK. Oops. What should have taken a
single stroke of the axe needed a lot of retakes.
Ouch. The first strike hit the back of her head
– and some in the crowd saw Mary's lips move.
The second thwack severed most of her neck,
but it took one final chop to complete the job.
The executioner held Mary's head up and
shouted, 'God save the Queen!' Oops again.
He was left holding her wig as her head fell
and rolled across the floor.

Squabbles and tiffs

The kings and queens of Europe were forever falling out with each other – often because of religion. Things got worse after the Reformation (from 1517), which tried to reform the Catholic Church. Many people and governments joined the new Protestant Church, while others kept faithful to the Catholic Church. That meant big rows, especially in Britain.

We bring you peace - unless you disagree with us.

Just for the record:

Henry VIII split the English Church away from the Pope, but this was mainly a row about his power. Henry remained a Catholic to the end of his life.

His son, Edward VI, was a Protestant.

Mary I tried to restore the Catholic Church – Protestants who disagreed were persecuted.

Elizabeth I did the opposite and persecuted Catholics. By the end of her reign England was a Protestant country.

James I was tolerant towards Catholics but introduced strict anti-Catholic laws after the Gunpowder Plot tried to blow him up.

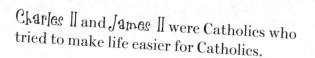

Charles I ended up fighting a civil war against Oliver Cromwell – who was a Puritan (a very strict Protestant and fierce enemy of Catholics).

Charles II and James II were Catholics who tried to make life easier for Catholics.

William III was a Protestant and took England to war to stop the Catholic French King Louis XIV from increasing his power.

Don't worry if you found that all very Confusing and baffling – so did they!

Queen Elizabeth I

Queen Elizabeth I died of old age, in 1603. She had proved to the world that a queen on the English throne could be powerful and respected by many. With her death, the Tudor dynasty came to an end, as she had no children to follow her. It was Queen Mary's son (King James VI of Scotland) who became king next, as James I of England.

And now for the Jacobean Era (Jacobus is Latin for James).

Foul fact:

King James was a bit of a stinker. He didn't have a lot of time for personal hygiene. Although the king, he wore the same clothes for months on end, even sleeping in them now and again. He also kept the same hat on 24/7 until it rotted to a frazzle. He refused to wash or bath as he was convinced it was bad for his health. What is it about royals and baths? Read on for more bathroom delights.

Furious French & revolting royals

Ooh la la, Louis.

We are so rich, ma chérie.

Through most of its history, France was ruled by kings. A lot of them were called Louis. Louis XIV (1638–1715) was probably the smelliest. His throne doubled as a toilet, and he sometimes used it while conducting court sessions. It was even said he would go to the toilet while driving a carriage. As if that wasn't foul enough, the king didn't take many baths in his life, partly because water was thought to carry disease (which it often did). Instead, he was rubbed down each day with cloths soaked in alcohol, so he probably reeked of body odour and brandy.

King Louis **XIV** made up for his stench by filling his rooms with flowers and dousing himself in perfume. In fact, he had a team of people design him a new perfume every week. He would also change his shirt three times a day – anything to avoid having a bath! Like his toilet habits, his dressing and undressing were public affairs. Every morning, the king called **100** men into his room to watch him while he got dressed. *Sacre bleu!*

I'm not smelly or crazy – just scent-a-mental.

Et voila, le limerick...

As he squatted, King Louis forebode;
How his royal accomplishments flowed...
The court had to stop
For each trickle and plop
While his throne doubled-up
as commode
(So that regal affairs could download).

Look out — it gets worse...

The French kings and queens lived at the Palace of Versailles, which was very grand but rather poor on toilets. There just weren't enough for all the staff and guests. The servants, commoners who came to see their monarch and even important guests would sometimes have to relieve themselves in corners and courtyards. No wonder Versailles was known for its foul smells. The problem became so bad that Louis XIV insisted the hallways had to be cleaned of poo once a week. *Quelle horreur!*

Marie Antoinette, Queen of France (1755–1793) didn't take many baths, either – about once a month, but she made quite a display of it. The water in the bathtub was scented and filled with sweet pine nuts, blanched sweet almonds, marshmallow root, lily bulbs and a paste of rare plants. That's quite a fancy bubble bath. She probably smelled fresh(ish) for the first few days afterwards, but by the end of the month she was bound to be smelling disgusting. No wonder things in Paris got revolting…

C'est la révolution!

The French Revolution

The French Revolution came when the people of France got rid of their powerful monarchy and took control of the government for themselves. The revolution lasted 10 years from 1789 to 1799. France was suffering famine and hardship, with many people struggling to survive. The cost of bread rocketed and people starved, while the royals lived in luxury at public expense.

Thousands of rich people were executed by guillotine, including Queen Marie Antoinette and King Louis XVI in 1793. France then became a republic (where a government has a chief of state who is not a monarch and who is usually an elected president).

The final words of Marie Antoinette were said to be, 'Pardonnez-moi, Monsieur'. The doomed queen was apologising to her executioner for stepping on his foot by mistake on her way to the guillotine.

It must be time for gateau – there's a huge cake-slicer.

A revolutionary joke

At the height of the French Revolution a royal footman, a lady in waiting and the palace caretaker are all to be put to death by the guillotine. The footman stoops down, places his neck over the frame and waits for the blade to fall. The blade shudders and drops, but judders to a stop just millimetres from his neck. The executioner announces that the footman can't be legally executed twice, so they let him go free.

The lady in waiting goes next and exactly the same thing happens. The blade judders to a stop millimetres from her neck. Everyone watching agrees she was saved by some kind of higher power, so they let her go free. The palace caretaker is next. He stares up at the blade and suddenly shouts as he takes an oil can from his pocket, 'Wait a second, I see your problem...'

It's a shame the guillotine didn't cut that joke.

Valiant Victoria

Queen Victoria (1819–1901)

Some of Britain's queens have been remarkable for the length of their reigns, as well as for the amazing events through which they ruled. Queen Victoria set a record for her long reign (1838–1901) and also for the size of her realm – when the British Empire stretched across many parts of the world.

With a reign of 63 years, 7 months and 2 days, Victoria was the longest-reigning British monarch and the longest-reigning queen in world history until her great-great-granddaughter Elizabeth II beat her record on 9th September 2015.

Cheesy fact

When Queen Victoria married Prince Albert, she received a giant cheddar cheese as a wedding gift. The huge block of cheese weighed over 500 kilograms and was made from the milk of 750 cows. The queen accepted the present and put it on display. After the exhibition she refused to take the cheese back. How ungrateful! (Yes, it would be a real grater-full.)

I just don't know what to do with it.

Hard cheese - you're in a pickle. Look after it Caerphilly.

Did you know?

Queen Victoria's life was threatened at least seven times. In 1840, a man tried to shoot the Queen because he didn't think England should be ruled by a woman. In 1872 an Irishman with a pistol tried to get her to sign a document that would free the Irish from the English.

As if that wasn't scary enough for her, Queen Victoria and Prince Albert had nine children, but she hated having babies and thought breastfeeding was disgusting. She called babies 'nasty objects' and 'frog-like'.

Victoria was really strict with her children and didn't show them much love. Her eldest son, Bertie (later King Edward VII), was a big disappointment to her and she thought of him as an ugly halfwit. One day Prince Albert went to see Bertie to sort him out and they took a walk in the rain. Prince Albert came back feeling unwell and died three weeks later. Queen Victoria blamed Bertie for the death of her beloved husband for the rest of her life.

Knicker alert

When Queen Victoria's extraordinarily large bloomers were auctioned in 2015, the world watched in horror. How could a woman who weighed so little on her wedding day have ended up filling such massive underwear? It was all down to her diet, especially as she got older and piled on the pounds. At the age of 18, the slender monarch insisted on 'eating like a Queen', feasting on all kinds of fattening delights. As an old lady, she tended to bolt down her food and suffered from terrible indigestion and a fair amount of royal flatulence.

Did I hear the royal trumpeter or was it something else?

Foul joke

Queen Victoria was showing the Archbishop of Canterbury around the royal stable, when one of the stallions close by broke wind so loudly it couldn't be ignored. 'Oh dear,' said the Queen, 'How embarrassing. I'm frightfully sorry about that.'

'It's quite understandable,' said the Archbishop, 'as a matter of fact I thought it was the horse.'

Limerick

At breakfast, the Queen looked confused

At a king-sized egg, which she refused.

'It's huge to EGGcess,

From an ostrich, I'd guess.

In fact,' she frowned,

'I'm just not EMUsed.'

Did you know?

The Penny Black was the world's first postage stamp used in a public postal system. It was first issued in Great Britain on 1 May 1840. It features a profile of Queen Victoria facing left. Rare Victorian Penny Blacks are valued at tens of thousands of pounds today.

Cue for another limerick:

The queen was approached by a tramp,
And the back of her head
became damp
When he licked her and slobbered,
Before he got clobbered...
He'd thought that her face
was a stamp!

LAST

cheesy jokes

Once upon a time...

Once upon a time, a beautiful princess saw a frog hop from the royal pond. The frog looked up at her and croaked, 'I once was a handsome prince until an evil witch put a spell on me. One kiss from you and I will turn back into a prince . Then we can marry and move into the castle with my mother, the Queen. You can look after us, cook our meals, clean all the state rooms, entertain our guests, wear a crown and forever be at my side to smile sweetly and always be grateful.' The princess smiled as sweetly as she could. That night, she dined alone… on the finest frog's legs on toast she'd ever eaten.

Give me a kiss and I'll treat you to dinner.

A long joke

A king who enjoyed fishing called the royal forecaster and asked about the weather for the next few hours. The weatherman assured him there was no chance of rain. So the king and queen set off to go salmon fishing in the hills.

On the way they met a farmer with his donkey. On seeing the king and queen, the farmer said, 'Your Majesties, you should return to the palace at once because any minute now it's going to pour with rain.'

The king smiled and said, "My royal weatherman has assured me all will be fine. He is very clever and I pay him very high wages. He gave me a different forecast. I trust him so we will continue on our way." So they did.

Very shortly, a downpour beat down on them and thunder shook the ground. The king and queen were totally soaked. Furious, the king returned to the palace and gave the order to fire the weatherman at once. Then he summoned the farmer and offered him the job of royal weather forecaster.

My donkey's called Gale as she's an expert on wind.

The farmer said, 'Your Majesty, I do not know anything about forecasting. I get my information from my donkey. If I see my donkey's ears drooping, it means it will rain. If its tail rises, we are in for wind. If it nods its head, we're due for fine weather.' So instead, the King hired the donkey on the spot – as chief adviser.

And so began the practice of hiring asses to work in government to occupy its chief positions!

And finally:

Quotes from the British Monarchy – The Windsors

On a walkabout in Scotland, Queen Elizabeth II heard someone say that she looked just like the Queen. Her Majesty quickly replied, 'How reassuring'.

'I learned the way a monkey learns – by watching its parents.' Prince Charles

117

'As I learned from growing up, you don't mess with your grandmother.' Prince William

'If it doesn't fart or eat hay, she's not interested.' Prince Philip, about his daughter Princess Anne, a keen horse rider.

If you survived some of the truly foul facts and cheesy jokes in this book, take a look at the other wacky titles in this revolting series. They're all guaranteed to make you groan and squirm like never before. Share them with your friends AT YOUR OWN RISK!

QUIZ

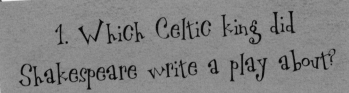

1. Which Celtic king did Shakespeare write a play about?

a) King Kong

b) King MacDonald

c) King Lear

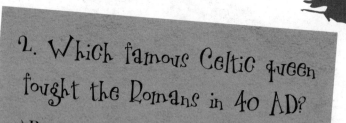

2. Which famous Celtic queen fought the Romans in 40 AD?

a) Beyoncé

b) Boudicca

c) Beatrix

3. Who did Queen Juana I of Castile marry?

a) Philip the Handsome of Austria

b) Louis the Ugly of France

c) Eric the Hunk of Finland

4. Who was the main villain in traditional Robin Hood tales?

a) King John

b) Macbeth

c) Voldemort

5. How did James II of Scotland die?

a) His head was chopped off

b) He strained too hard on the toilet

c) He was blown up by a cannon backfiring

6. What happened to Henry VIII's second wife, Anne Boleyn?

a) He divorced her

b) He had her beheaded

c) She died having a baby

7. Who was the last Tudor queen?

a) Queen Elizabeth I

b) Queen Mary I

c) Queen Victoria I

Would you serve in my court? I fancy a game of tennis.

8. Who did Charles I fight a Civil war against?

a) Richard Cromwell

b) Oliver Cromwell

c) Captain America

9. Which monarch's throne doubled as a toilet?

a) Louis XIV

b) Queen Ranavalona I

c) Henry VIII

10. Who was Queen Victoria's husband?

a) Prince Albert

b) Prince Philip

c) Prince Harry

Answers:

1 = c
2 = b
3 = a
4 = a
5 = c
6 = b
7 = a
8 = b
9 = a
10 = a

GLOSSARY

Arsenic: a very poisonous chemical, usually a white powder having no smell.

Catholic Church: a branch of the Christian church with the Pope as its head.

Celts: people who lived in Britain and northwest Europe during the Iron Age from 600 BC to 43 AD, when the Romans arrived in Britain.

Earl: a type of British nobleman.

Guillotine: a machine with a heavy blade, which was used for beheading people.

Monarchy: a type of government of a country with a head of state who inherits the position, rules for life and holds various powers.

Protestant Church: a branch of the Christian church which was developed in the 16th century by Christians who disliked the Catholic Church.

Vikings: people from Scandinavia who invaded Britain and other parts of Europe from the late 700s to the 1000s AD.